Paige, Lilah, Kassi,
Basically
This belongs
to the Svatek
Family.

ARCTURUS

This edition published in 2016 by Arcturus Publishing Limited
26/27 Bickels Yard, 151–153 Bermondsey Street,
London SE1 3HA

Illustrations: Fabio Santomaro
Designer: Trudi Webb
Editor: Joe Harris
Authors: Sally Lindley and Joe Fullman

ISBN 978-1-78428-211-0
CH004986NT
Supplier: 29, Date 0716, Print run 5319

Printed in China

CONTENTS

What has 99 legs and one eye?

A pirate centipede!

What's the difference between a buffalo and a cookie?

You can't dunk a buffalo in your milk!

What's wet, striped, and goes bump-bump?

A zebra in a clothes dryer!

Why did the polar bear return some food to the supermarket?

Because the seal was broken!

WHY CAN'T YOU TRUST THE KING OF THE JUNGLE?

Because he's always lion!

What do you call an explosive ape?

A baboom!

What do you call a lion that runs a photocopier?

A copycat!

How do you become a marsupial?

You have to have the right koalafications!

Why did the hippo go to the doctor?

It was a hippochondriac!

What do you get if you cross a snake with a builder?

A boa constructor!

What game do jellyfish play at parties?

Tide-and-seek!

Why couldn't the frog put down the book it was reading?

It was just too ribbit-ing!

What did the lion say when the zookeeper stopped it from eating a famous poet?

You took the words right out of my mouth!

Little snake: Mama, are we poisonous?

Mama: No, dear, why?

Little snake: I just bit my lip!

What do you call an empty bowl of parrot food?

Polly-gone!

What toy did the baby snake have?

A rattle!

What did the doctor give to the nervous elephant?

Pills to keep him trunkquil!

What do you call a reindeer with no eyes?

No eye-deer!

What do you call a reindeer with no eyes or legs?

Still no eye-deer!

What kind of fast food do polar bears like best?

Ice-burgers!

What do you call a hairdressing competition for lions?

The mane event!

Why did the sickly crab walk sideways?

Its medicine had side effects!

Why wouldn't the oyster twins share?

Because they were two shellfish!

What did the porcupine say when her son sat on her knee?

Ouch!

WHAT KIND OF BEARS STAND IN THE RAIN?

Drizzly bears!

What do baby camels drink in the desert?

Evaporated milk!

Why don't anteaters get ill?

Because they're full of anty-bodies!

What did the aquatic mammal say when it left the party?

I'm otter here!

What did the whale do when it watched a sad movie?

It started to blubber!

What's big, furry, and flies?

A hot-air baboon!

WHY DO SKUNKS argue a Lot?

Because they like to raise a stink!

How does the king of the jungle spend his days off?

Just lion around!

Did you hear about the hippo at the North Pole?

It got hippothermia!

Did you hear about the elephant that doesn't matter?

It's an irrelephant.

Why do flamingos stand on one leg?

Because if they stood on no legs, they'd fall over!

What kind of dance do elephants do best?

The Stomp!

What's the easiest way to catch a fish?

Ask someone to throw it to you!

What do you call a bear with no ears?

A "B"!

What time do ducks get up?

At the quack of dawn!

How does a hippo get to school?

On the hippopotabus!

What do you call a monkey with a scar and a wand?

Hairy Potter!

Why are camels so good at hide-and-seek?

Because of their camel-flage!

Where do you find giant snails?

On the end of giants' toes!

Which bird is very rude?

A mockingbird!

WHAT DO YOU GET IF YOU CROSS A POLAR BEAR WITH A HARP?

A bear-faced lyre!

What did the lion say as it watched the bike race?

Meals on wheels!

What did one frog say to the other?

Time's sure fun when you're having flies!

Did you hear about the rich spiders that got married?

They had an elaborate webbing!

How do you find the best marsupials?

Look for the ones with the best koalaties!

What did the insect say before it tried a bungee jump?

Earwig-o!

WHY CAN'T WHALES BE TRUSTED?

Because they're all blubbermouths!

Which birds steal soap from the bathroom?

Robber ducks!

What do you get if you cross a parrot and an elephant?

An animal that tells you everything it remembers!

What do cheetahs eat?

Fast food!

What did the llama say when it was invited to visit Spain?

Alpaca my suitcase!

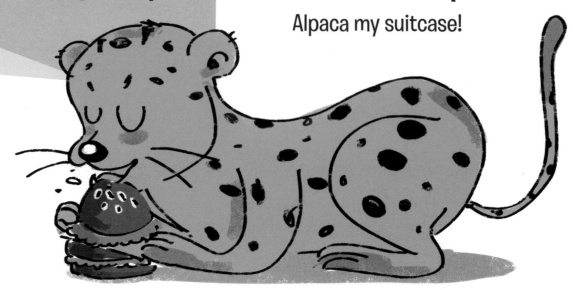

What's the fastest way for a reindeer to travel?

By icicle!

Why did the birds cry when they heard the story about the peacock?

Because it's such a beautiful tale!

What do you call a kangaroo when it's asleep?

Out of bounds!

Which of Jack Sparrow's feathered friends live in the jungle?

The Parrots of the Caribbean!

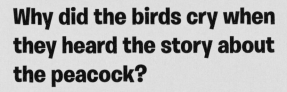

Why do bears have fur coats?

Because they'd look silly in jackets!

WHY DON'T TUNA PLAY TENNIS?
They don't want to get caught in the net!

Where did the leopard have its picnic?
It found just the right spot!

What do you call a kangaroo at the North Pole?
A lost-tralian!

What type of socks do bears wear?
They don't, they have bear feet!

How do you greet a marine mammal?
Whale, hello!

Why do birds fly south in the winter?

Because it's too far to walk!

What's the difference between a coyote and a flea?

One howls on the prairie, the other prowls on the hairy!

What's yellow and black with red spots?

A leopard with acne!

Why was the baby ant confused?

Because all his uncles were ants!

Which jungle creature tells the best jokes?

A stand-up chameleon!

HOW DO YOU GET A HiPPO tO FOLLOW ORDERS?

Put it under hippo-nosis!

How do bees brush their hair?

They use a honey comb!

What do you call a bug that's see-through?

A glasshopper!

What did the TV presenter say when he saw a herd of buffalo coming over the hill?

Look, there's a herd of buffalo coming over the hill!

What did the TV presenter say when he saw a herd of wildebeest coming over the hill?

And now for some gnus ...

How do apes make cheese sandwiches?

They gorilla them!

What does a toucan wear to go swimming?

A beak-ini!

What do you get if you cross a centipede and a parrot?

A walkie-talkie!

Which legendary concert did cows go to in the 1960s?

Livestock!

Why don't birds of prey like parties? They feel hawkward!

What's the best job for a spider?

Web designer!

What did the baby dolphin shout when it got caught in seaweed?

Kelp!

How many skunks does it take to make a really, really bad smell?

A phew!

Which spotted wild cat is angriest?

The cross-alot!

BUT WHICH SPOTTED WILD CAT IS THE MOST EXPENSIVE?

The cost-alot!

Why do penguins carry fish in their beaks?

Because they don't have any pockets!

What do seagulls tell their children before bed?

Ferry tales!

Why shouldn't you believe what fleas and ticks tell you?

They're all lice.

What's green and slimy and found in the ocean?

Whale snot!

What do you get if you spill birdseed in your shoes?

Pigeon toes!

What do you call a fly with no wings?

A walk!

How does a penguin travel across the ice?

It just goes with the floe!

Why are salmon easy to weigh?

Because they have their own scales!

How did the wildebeest get down the river?

It paddled its own gnu!

WHY DIDN'T THE PENGUIN GET MARRIED?

Because it got cold feet!

What's the most common music in the jungle?

Snake, rattle, and roll!

What was the turtle doing on the racetrack?

About ten inches an hour!

What do giraffes have that no other animal has?

Baby giraffes!

Did you hear about the stranded polar bear?

It was ice-olated!

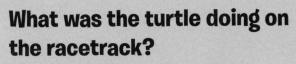

How would you describe a chicken that's really good at eating?

Im-peck-able!

WHY DID THE LION EAT THE STILT WALKER?

It wanted a well-balanced meal!

Did you hear about the cannibal lion?

He had to swallow his pride!

What's small, cuddly, and purple?

A koala holding its breath!

Knock knock.

Who's there?

Cows go.

Cows go who?

Cows go "moo" not "who!"

How do cats say goodbye to each other?

Have a mice day!

Which bird is most commonly seen near a temple?

A bird of pray!

What is green but turns red when you flick the switch?

A frog in a blender!

What do you call a camel without any humps?

Humphrey!

What do you get if you cross a baby and a porcupine?

Problems when it's time to give her a bath!

What do you call a man who lives with a pack of wolves?

Wolfgang.

Why did the sick frog visit a hospital?

He needed a hop-eration!

Why shouldn't you talk to rabbits about vegetables?

Because they don't carrot all!

Why don't cheetahs wash?

They don't want to be spotless!

What do you get if you cross a parrot and a lion?

A bird that talks your head off!

WHAT'S WORSE THAN A BULL IN A CHINA SHOP?

A porcupine in a balloon factory!

How do you start a firefly race?

On your marks, get set, glow!

Where do meerkats keep their money?

In sandbanks!

Did you hear about the rhino that caught a cold?

It became a rhi-snot-eros!

What do insects use to stop them from smelling?

Deodor-ant!

WHAT SHOULD a LIZARD DO iF it LOSES its tail?

Go to a retail outlet!

What do you call two matching penguins?

Pengtwins!

Why do giraffes have such long necks?

Because their feet smell!

What happened to the lion that spent Christmas by the ocean?

It got sandy claws!

Did you hear about the two silkworms that ran a race?

They ended up in a tie!

How do fish get home from parties?

By taxi crab!

What's brown and dangerous and lives in a tree?

A monkey with a carton of eggs!

What did the small fish say after a business meeting?

Let minnow what you think!

Why did the fish take a weekend break?

Just for the halibut!

What do you call a really, really old ant?

An antique!

How do porcupines play leapfrog?

Extremely carefully!

What's the best time to buy a canary?

When it's going cheep!

Why did the reindeer run around in circles?

Because it was in Lapland!

Why couldn't the butterfly go to the dance?

It was a moth ball!

WHAT'S BLACK AND WHITE AND RED ALL OVER?

A sunburned zebra!

What do polar bears do when they're not hunting?

They just chill!

If you keep fish in an aquarium and plants in a terrarium, what do you keep pandas in?

A panda-monium!

What do you get if you cross a snake with a pig?

A boar constrictor!

What goes grrr, squelch, grrr, squelch?

A lion in soggy shoes!

What do you call a dead skunk? Ex-stinked!

WHY are elephants always Late for the plane?

Because they take so long to pack their trunks!

Why did the tiger cheat on its homework?

Because it was a copycat!

What do you get if you cross a cat and a parrot?

A carrot!

Why do monkeys love bananas so much?

They're so a-peeling!

Why do skunks know a lot about the past?

Because they have a real scents of history!

Why are cats slow readers?

Because they paws after every claws!

What do you call a tiger that has eaten your dad's sister?

An aunt-eater!

Why did the joey get on his mother's nerves?

He kept jumping on his bed!

What's the difference between a tiger and a lion?

A tiger has the mane part missing!

WHAT DID THE MACAW SAY TO THE TOUCAN?

Talk is cheep!

Where do you usually find sloths?

It depends where you left them!

What's the medical term for a parrot that has lost its memory?

Polynesia!

What's the best way to get in touch with a fish?

Drop them a line!

What is large and has three trunks?

An elephant going abroad!

WHAT DO YOU CALL TWIN PORCUPINES? A prickly pair!

36

WHAT DO YOU CALL A FLYING SKUNK?

A smellycopter!

Where do basking sharks keep their belongings?

On the continental shelf!

What did the rabbit say to the carrot?

It's been nice gnawing you!

How did the bird with a broken wing stop itself falling from the sky?

It used its sparrowchute!

Why wasn't the firefly mother happy?

Because her children weren't very bright!

WHAT DID THE LOBSTER SAY TO HER HUSBAND?

Stop being so snappy!

Why shouldn't elephants visit the beach?

In case their trunks fall down!

Why are bears so clumsy when they dance?

Because they have two left feet!

Where do birds go in the evenings?

To a crowbar!

Why are tropical birds good at tennis?

Because toucan play at that game!

Why did the jellyfish cross the ocean?

To get to the other tide!

What's the biggest danger for fishermen?

Pulling a mussel!

How do dolphins decide who goes first?

Flipper coin!

What did the horse say when it fell over?

"I can't giddy-up!"

What weighs 10 tons and squirts custard at you?

An elephant eating a doughnut!

How do you stop a skunk from smelling?

Hold its nose!

Did you hear about the snake's valentine?

He sealed it with a hiss!

What does a builder use to fix the ape house at the zoo?

A monkey wrench!

How do bees celebrate moving to a new place?

With a house-swarming party!

Where do sharks go for the winter?

Finland!

What weighs a ton and floats gracefully through the air?

A hang-gliding rhinoceros!

Where do whales go to watch a movie?

To the dive-in!

Did you hear about the cobras who fought?

They eventually hissed and made up!

Which day do spiders look forward to?

Webs-day!

Why are skunks good at understanding things?

Because they have a lot of common scents!

Did you hear about the snake that swallowed some keys?

It got lockjaw!

What do you get if you cross a herd of elephants with a cargo of prunes?

Out of the way!

What do you get if you cross a shark and an elephant?

Swimming trunks!

What did one snake say to the other snake when they split up?

Fangs for the memory!

DID YOU HEAR ABOUT THE SEA CREATURE THAT MADE iT BiG IN HOLLYWOOD?

It was a starfish!

Which fish do builders like best?

Hammerhead sharks!

Did you hear about it raining cats and dogs?

There were poodles all over the road!

Did you hear about the other time it rained cats and dogs?

Well, as long as it doesn't reindeer!

What kind of fish does a parrot like best?

A perch!

What does an octopus wear to keep it warm?

A coat of arms!

WHAT DiD THE FROG SAY WHEN it SaW THE TOAD?

Wart's new?

Which side of a porcupine is the prickliest?

The outside!

Why do hummingbirds hum?

Because they don't know the words!

What did the lion cub say to its mother?

Every day I love you roar and roar!

What sound does an alpaca's doorbell make?

Llama-llama-ding-dong!

Which TV show do cockatiels enjoy?

The feather forecast!

Why did the pigs stop sunbathing?

Because they were bacon in the heat!

Why wouldn't the hyena play cards with the other animals?

Because one was a cheetah, and the other was lion!

What music do fish like best?

Sole music!

What does an octopus use to cut something in half?

A sea-saw!

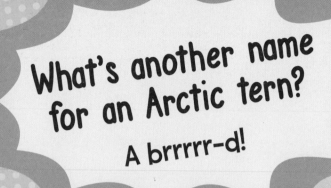

What's another name for an Arctic tern?

A brrrrr-d!

What do you call an alligator that works for the police?

An investi-gator!

Why do divers approach octopuses very carefully?

Because they're heavily armed!

Why do baby snakes stay close to their parents?

Because a boa's best friend is his smother!

WHAT HAUNTS GRAVEYARDS IN AFRICA?

Elephantoms!

What's yellow, sweet, and is found in the jungle?
Tarzipan!

How did the French fries get engaged?
With an onion ring!

How did the joke about the peanut butter become so popular?
I guess it must have spread!

What do refuse collectors like to eat?
Junk food!

WHAT'S THE BEST THING TO PUT INTO A PIE? Your teeth.

What did the egg say to the whisk?

I know when I'm beaten!

What are the strongest vegetables?

Muscle sprouts.

Did you hear about the paranoid orange?

He always kept his eyes peeled for danger!

Which vegetable do dogs like best?

The collie-flower!

What did the fast tomato say to the slow tomato?

Come on, ketchup!

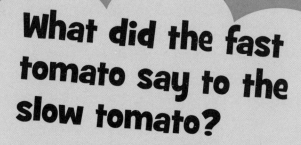

What did the cucumber say to the carrot?

Want to go for a dip?

Shakespeare walked into a diner and asked for a drink.

The man behind the counter shook his head and said, "You're Bard."

Why couldn't the farmer water his garden?

There was a leek in his bucket!

Knock knock!

Who's there?

Dishes.

Dishes who?

Dishes me. Who's that?

WHAT DO YOU GET IF YOU PUT THREE DUCKS IN A BOX?

A box of quackers!

What do you call shoes made out of bananas?
Slippers!

Why did dinosaurs eat raw meat?
They didn't know how to cook!

How do parrots drink?
Out of a beak-er!

Why shouldn't you put a lot of fungi in a stew?

Because there isn't mush-room!

Why won't you starve on a desert island?

Because of the sand which is there (sandwiches there).

If apples come from an apple tree, and oranges come from an orange tree, where do chickens come from?

A poul-tree.

What do you call a gingerbread man with a degree?

A smart cookie!

What did one knife say to the other?

Look sharp!

DID YOU HEAR ABOUT THE CANNIBAL WEDDING?

They toasted the bride and groom!

What do you call a bear with no teeth?

A gummy bear!

Which bird turns up at every mealtime?

A swallow!

What do you call cheese that belongs to someone else?

Nacho cheese!
(Not your cheese.)

What is green and sings?

Elvis Parsley!

What's red and dangerous?

Shark-infested tomato soup!

WHAT DID ONE SNOWMAN SAY TO THE OTHER?

Can you smell carrots?

What do birds grow on?

Egg plants!

Knock knock!

Who's there?

Lettuce.

Lettuce who?

Lettuce in, and you'll find out!

Knock knock!

Who's there?

Carla.

Carla who?

Carla restaurant, I'm hungry!

Did you hear about the gravy that giggled?

It was made with laughing stock!

Why didn't the almonds go to the ballet?
Because they were afraid of The Nutcracker!

How do you make a walnut laugh?
Crack it up!

Waiter, there's a dead fly swimming in my soup!
Don't be silly, madam. Dead flies can't swim.

How do comedians like their eggs cooked?
Funny-side up!

What do you get if you cross a snake and an apple tart?
A pie-thon!

What did the cannibal order at the restaurant?

Pizza with everyone on it!

What kind of dog doesn't have a tail?

A hot dog!

What type of ice cream do birds like the most?

Chocolate chirp!

Where do baby cows go for lunch?

The calf-eteria!

WHAT DO MONSTERS PUT IN THEIR SANDWICHES?

Scream cheese!

How do you fit an elephant in the fridge?

Open the door, and push it really hard!

How do you fit a giraffe in the fridge?

Take the elephant out first!

Why shouldn't you tease egg whites?

Because they can't take a yolk!

If you divide a marshmallow in half and then in half again, what do you get?

Really sticky fingers!

Why did the walnut go out with a raisin?

It couldn't find a date!

WHAT DID SUSHI A say to SUSHI B?

"Wasabi?"
(What's up, B?)

Why did the truck driver stop for a snack?

He saw a fork in the road!

Why did the farmer work his field with a steamroller?

He wanted to grow mashed potatoes!

Why did the tofu cross the road?

To prove it wasn't chicken!

Why did the potato cry?

Someone had hurt its peelings!

Did you hear about the banana that went to charm school?

He turned into a real smoothie!

If you had 5 hens, 4 geese, and 6 ducks, what would you have?

Lots of eggs!

What would happen if pigs could fly?

The price of bacon would go up!

What does a penguin have in its salad?

Iceberg lettuce!

WHICH DRINK DO FROG'S ENJOY?

Croak-a-cola!

Knock knock!

Who's there?

Doughnut.

Doughnut who?

Doughnut ask, it's a secret.

Why was the mushroom invited to a lot of parties?

He was a fun-gi to be with!

What do you call someone who loves hot chocolate?

A cocoa-nut!

Which dessert is never on time?

Choco-late brownies!

What's white, sweet, and lives in the jungle?

A meringue-utan!

Why do seagulls fly over the sea?

Because if they flew over a bay, they'd be bagels!

Why did the gardener quit her job?

Because her celery wasn't high enough!

Which food do mathematicians like best?

Square-root vegetables!

Waiter, there's a twig in my meal!

Just a moment, sir, I'll get the branch manager.

WHERE DID THE SPAGHETTI GO TO DANCE?

To a meatball!

What kind of insect do you get if you throw butter out the window?

A butter-fly!

Which salad is the best at playing pool?

The cue-cumber!

What's orange and sounds like a parrot?

A carrot!

What did the nut say when it had a cold?

Cashew!

Did you hear about the numbskull who ate a light bulb?

He said he only wanted a light meal.

Knock knock!

Who's there?

Olive.

Olive who?

Olive just across the street from you.

What do you call an egg that plays tricks on people?

A practical yolker.

What cheese is made backward?

Edam!

What did the newspaper say to the ice cream?

Hey, what's the scoop?

Waiter, do you have frog's legs?

No, madam, I always walk like this.

Knock knock!
Who's there?
Emma.
Emma who?
Emma going to have my dinner now?

Knock knock!
Who's there?
Figs.
Figs who?
Figs the doorbell. My hand hurts from all the knocking.

What famous city is known as the Big Egg?
New Yolk City!

WAITER, WHAT IS THIS SPIDER DOING ON MY ICE CREAM?
I don't know, madam. Skiing, maybe?

Why shouldn't you cycle to school on an empty stomach?

Because it's easier on a bicycle.

What does bread do after it comes out of the oven?

It loafs around!

Did you hear about the cabbage whose friend won the lottery?

He was green with envy!

Waiter, what's this?

It's bean soup, sir.

I don't care what it's been. What is it now?

What do you get if you cross a pig and a dinosaur?

Jurassic Pork!

What do you call a cheese that surrounds a castle?

Moat-zarella!

How does a penguin make pancakes?

With its flippers!

Teacher: Name four things that contain milk.

Student: Yogurt, butter, cheese, and ... the truck from the dairy.

What vegetable are sailors scared of?

Leeks!

Waiter, there are flies in my soup!

Yes, sir, I think it's the rotten meat that attracts them.

What do you call a peanut in space?

An astro-nut!

Why did the farmer send his cows to the gym every day?

He wanted low-fat milk!

Why did the cook keep putting the peas through a colander?

He had a re-straining order!

Waiter, this lettuce tastes like soap.

I should hope so, madam, I just washed it.

Why did mother grape go on a spa retreat?

She was tired of raisin kids!

HOW DO YOU MAKE GOLDEN SOUP?

Put 24 carrots in it!

What kind of fruit has a bad temper?

A crab apple!

Waiter, do you serve lobsters here?

Yes, sir, we serve anybody.

Why did the chewing gum cross the road?

Because it was stuck to the chicken's foot!

What did the penguin order at the Mexican restaurant?

Brrr-itos!

Why did the teapot get in trouble?

Because it was naught-tea!

Why did the grape stop in the middles of the road?

He ran out of juice!

Why did the man eat his lunch at the bank?

He loved rich food!

Teacher: Do you eat French fries with your fingers?

Student: No, I usually eat them with burgers.

Why shouldn't you tell jokes to eggs?

Because they might crack up!

Waiter, there's a wasp in my soup!
I think you'll find it's a vitamin bee, sir.

What do you call a potato standing by the Eiffel Tower?

A French fry!

What do owls eat for breakfast?

Mice krispies!

Waiter, I think I just swallowed a fish bone!

Are you choking?

No, I'm serious!

WHAT DRINK DO SOCCER PLAYERS LIKE LEAST?

Penal-tea!

Where do milkshakes come from?

Dancing cows!

Where's the best place to store pizza?

In your stomach!

Where do cats prepare their meals?

The kit-chen!

Why did the girl stare at the carton of juice?

Because it said "concentrate."

What happened to the nutmeg that got arrested?

It ended up in custardy!

WHAT PIZZA TOPPING DO ANTEATERS LIKE BEST?

Ant-chovies!

Why do horses eat every day at the same time?

Because they need a stable diet!

Where do ice cream sellers learn their trade?

At Sundae school.

Why did the boy give mustard to his poodle when it had a fever?

Hot dogs are always better with mustard!

Why couldn't the sesame seed stop cracking jokes?

It was on a roll!

What do owls eat at the seaside?

Mice cream!

How do you get a mouse to smile?

Say cheese!

When is the best time to pick apples?

When the farmer is away from home!

Why did the baker work overtime?

She kneaded the dough!

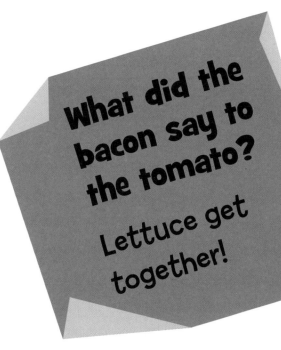

What did the bacon say to the tomato?

Lettuce get together!

Waiter, there's an ant in my soup!

I know, madam. The flies stay away during the winter.

How do you know that an elephant has raided your fridge?

There are footprints in the cheesecake!

Why didn't the large man know he was overweight?

It just kind of snacked up on him!

What do they eat at birthday parties in heaven?

Angel food cake!

WHAT KIND OF KEY OPENS A BANANA?

A mon-key!

Waiter, what is this fly doing in my soup?

Well madam, it looks like the backstroke.

What do you say to bees who try to steal honey?
Oh, beehive yourself!

Waiter, there's a slug in my salad!
Don't worry, sir, we won't charge extra.

Which hotel do mice stay in?
The Stilton!

Did you hear about the angry pancake?
It just flipped!

What do dogs eat at the movies?
Pup-corn!

Why did the pig kidnap the farmer?
To save his own bacon!

What meal do atomic scientists like best?
Nuclear fission chips!

Waiter, I can't eat this food. Please call the manager.
It's no use, madam, he can't eat it either.

Why did the farmer think the chicken had stolen his dinner?

He suspected fowl play!

What kind of people eat snails?

Ones who don't like fast food!

Why did the baker stop making doughnuts?

He was bored of the hole business!

What do you call someone that takes her own salt and pepper everywhere she travels?

A seasoned tourist!

What's the worst thing about being an octopus?

Washing your hands before dinner.

What should you do if your chicken smells funny?

Don't eat it, it's fowl!

Waiter, will the pizza be long?

No, it will be round!

Why did the boy eat a cupcake each night before bed?

So he could have sweet dreams!

What's a dog's top sweet treat?

Pup-tarts!

WHAT KIND OF CHEESE DO YOU USE TO LURE A BEAR AWAY?

Camembert!
("Come on bear!")

What's small, round, white, and giggles?

A tickled onion!

How did the egg get up the mountain?

It scrambled!

What did the martial artist buy from the butcher?

Karate chops!

Waiter, there is a spider on my plate. Call the manager at once!

That won't do any good, sir. She's afraid of them, too.

When are you allowed to take bubblegum to school?

On chews-day!

WHAT DO YOU CALL A REALLY LARGE PUMPKIN?

A plumpkin!

What do snowmen eat for breakfast?

Frosted flakes!

Why don't people laugh at gardeners' jokes?

Because they're too corny!

How can you spell the name of a hungry insect using just three letters?

M. T. B.

When should you take a cookie to the doctor?

When it feels crummy!

Where do tomatoes hang out on Fridays?

The salad bar!

Why did the chef dream that his pillow was turkey?

Because they're both full of stuffing!

What do farmers wear to gather their crops?

A har-vest!

Why did the banana go to see the doctor?

Because it wasn't peeling well!

WHY COULDN'T THE TEDDY BEAR FINISH ITS LUNCH?

Because it was stuffed!

A cheeseburger walks into a diner and asks for orange juice.

The waiter says, "I'm sorry, we don't serve food here."

What do you get if you keep your toys in the fridge?

A teddy brrrrr!

What's the difference between ice cream and milk chocolate?

Anyone can scream, but no one can milk chocolate.

What's the difference between roast beef and pea soup?

Anyone can roast beef, but have you ever tried to pea soup?

Are carrots really good for your eyesight?

Well, have you ever seen a rabbit wearing glasses?

What do vegetarian spiders eat?

Corn on the cobweb!

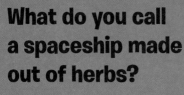

What do you call a spaceship made out of herbs?

A thyme machine!

How many more times do I have to tell you to walk away from the cupcakes?

None, I've eaten them all now!

Waiter, my plate is wet!

I think you'll find that's the soup.

Why did the basketball player always have cookies with his drink?

So he could dunk them!

Did you hear about the hilarious banana?
It had the whole fruit bowl in peels of laughter!

Knock knock!

Who's there?

June.

June who?

June know what time dinner is?

Why did the baker get fired from her job?

She was a loafer!

What starts with "T," ends with "T," and is full of "T"?

A teapot!

WHAT CAN YOU SERVE BUT NEVER EAT?

Tennis balls!

Why did the turkey join a band?

He had his own drumsticks!

Knock knock!

Who's there?

Ken.

Ken who?

Ken you get me something to eat? I'm starving.

Where do fish eat their dinners?

At a water table!

How do you make an apple turnover?

Push it downhill!

What do you call a man with his head in a saucepan?

Stu!

WHAT DID THE CAVEMAN ORDER FOR LUNCH?

A club sandwich!

How do you make a strawberry shake?

Put it in the freezer!

What did the spider order at the fast food restaurant?

A burger and flies!

Which fruit do twins like best?

Pears!

Did you hear about the cat that ate a lemon?

It was a sour puss!

Did you hear about
the peanut who kept
picking fights?

He was a-salted!

**Waiter, there's a
dead fly in my soup!**
Sorry, madam, are you
a vegetarian?

Why did the sausage roll?
Because it saw the milk shake!

What do astronauts eat out of?
Satellite dishes!

**No, but seriously,
what do astronauts
eat out of?**

Flying saucers!

What do you call spaghetti in disguise?

An impasta!

Waiter, this food tastes funny.

Then why aren't you laughing?

Waiter, is there pizza on the menu?

No, madam, I just wiped it off.

Knock knock!

Who's there?

Annie.

Annie who?

Annie chance of getting something to eat?

WHAT ARE LARGE, HAVE HORNS, AND GIVE MILK?

Dairy trucks!

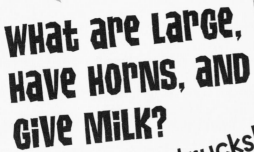

Why does Dracula wear lace-up shoes?
Because flip-flops look stupid with his tuxedo!

How do you get rid of stinky ghosts?
With scare freshener!

Which monster is horribly untidy?
The Loch Mess Monster!

How do you make a skeleton laugh?
Tickle its funny bone!

WHat are tHe BeSt MONSters tO aSK FOr DireCtiONS?
Where-wolves!

Grandma ogre: Did you pick your nose?

Little ogre: No, I was born with it!

What do vampires drink at night?

De-coffin-ated coffee!

What did the monster eat after his teeth were pulled?

The dentist!

What's the most important celebration in Egypt?

Mummy's Day!

What kind of music do mummies like? Wrap music!

Have you heard the monster comedian?

He's awfully funny!

What do you call a 12-foot monster with claws?

"Sir!"

Which dessert makes the swamp monster lick his lips?

Key slime pie!

Why is it difficult to tell twin witches apart?

Because you don't know which witch is which!

WHAT'S BLACK AND WHITE AND DEAD ALL OVER?

A zombie in a tuxedo!

Why didn't the skeleton go bungee jumping?

It didn't have the guts!

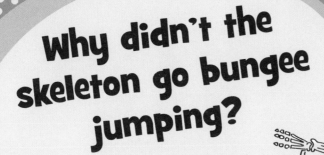

Why can you trust a mummy with your secrets?

They're good at keeping things under wraps!

Where did the zombie go to swim?

The Dead Sea!

Where did the zombie's best friend live?

Rotter-dam!

What's the difference between a dragon and a newspaper?

Have you ever tried to swat a fly with a dragon?

What does an ogre drive?
A monster truck!

What did the ogre say when he saw his friend's monster truck?

I'm green with envy!

What did the ghost write in his girlfriend's valentine card?

You're simply boo-tiful!

What do you call a monster who is kind to children?

A failure!

WHAT'S THE BEST PLACE TO TALK TO A MONSTER?

From as far away as possible!

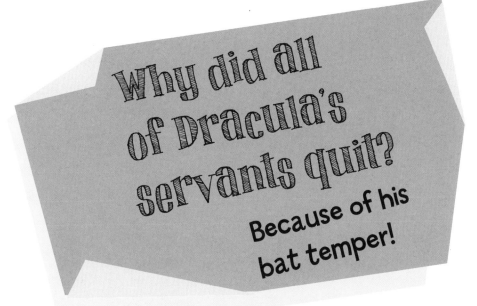

Why did all of Dracula's servants quit?

Because of his bat temper!

Why did the ancient Egyptian cross the road?

To get to his mummy!

What do you call an average-size troll?

Medi-ogre!

Why shouldn't you give green vegetables to evil monsters?

Because there's no peas for the wicked!

What do little vampires eat?

Alpha-bat soup!

WHY DID THE MONSTER STOP BITING HIS NAILS?

His mother said they might be rusty!

What did the little ghost say to his best friend?

"Do you believe in people?"

What are vampires most afraid of?

Tooth decay!

What is a vampire's best-loved sport?

Bat-minton!

How do you swap one witch for another?

Just add an "s" to make a switch!

Which extreme sport do monsters like best?

Fright-water rafting!

What do you say to a French skeleton?

Bone-jour!

What's green, has two heads and six arms, and goes "Beep, beep?"

An alien stuck in a traffic jam!

Why didn't the skeleton go to the party?

It didn't have any body to go with!

Who won the Zombie race?

No one, it was a dead heat!

Did you hear about the witch who turned green?

She got broom sick on long journeys!

Why is a yeti like an ox that's swallowed a stick of dynamite?

They're both abominable (a bomb in a bull).

Which monster is really good at science?

Frank Einstein!

How do monster stories begin?

"Once upon a slime ..."

WHY DID THE VAMPIRE NEED MOUTHWASH?

He had bat breath!

Who's the most important player on a monster soccer team?

The ghoul keeper!

Where do you rent a bloodsucking monster?

At a vamp-hire!

Which dance is hard for a vampire to resist?

The fang-dango!

How can you tell if an alien has used your hairbrush?

It glows in the dark!

What kind of monster loves to dance to pop music?

A boogie-man!

ON WHAT DAY DO Little MONSTers take a BaTH?

Scumday!

What's green, has two heads, and goes up and down?

An alien stuck in an elevator!

What type of dog does a vampire have?

A bloodhound!

On what day was the hairy monster born?

Fursday!

Which monster has one eye and one wheel?

A unicyclops!

Which meal do sea monsters like best?

Fish and ships!

Why did the monster buy three socks?

Because he grew three feet!

How does a zombie help you out?

He gives you a hand!

Why did Dracula take cold medicine?

To keep from coffin!

Why didn't the mummy have any friends?

He was too wrapped up in himself.

HOW CAN YOU TELL IF A SKELETON OWNS AN UMBRELLA?

It's bone dry!

How do witches race each other?

They ride vroomsticks!

Where's the safest place to hide from a zombie?

In the living room!

What do monsters eat at the beach?

Lice cream!

What do ghosts wash their hair with?

Sham-boo!

What did the skeleton order at the restaurant?

Spare ribs!

What does Dracula do in the summer?

He goes vamping!

How do monsters cook humans?

They like them terror-fried!

What kind of magic do witches perform using small plates?

Saucer-y!

What kind of books do ghosts read?

Whoooo done its!

Why did the banshee marry a pirate?

So she could wail the seven seas!

HOW DO YOU MAKE A WITCH JUMP?

Add a "t" to make them twitch.

When is it easy to beat a zombie in an argument?

When it has no leg to stand on!

What did ancient Egyptian monsters call their parents?

"Mummy and Deady"!

How did the monster spike its hair?

With scare gel!

What game do zombies like playing?

Hide-and-shriek!

What do you call a sprite with a twisted ankle?

A hobblin' goblin!

Did you hear about the ghost who was a big opera fan?

He loved haunting melodies!

What do you get if you cross an abominable snowman with a kangaroo?

A big fur coat with pockets!

Why did the cyclops' school close down?

Because it only had one pupil!

What kind of blood do pessimistic vampires like best?

B negative!

Why did the vampire take up acting?
It was in his blood!

Why do novelists like to write in cemeteries?
Because there are so many plots there!

What do monsters eat with their cake?
Eyes-cream!

WHERE DO BABY BANSHEES LEARN TO WAIL?
In noisery school!

How do you know the skull won the race?

It was definitely ahead!

How do you get into a haunted house?

With a skeleton key!

What do zombies play in the playground?

Corpses and robbers!

Why was Dracula thrown out of his art class?

He could only draw blood.

Why should you be especially afraid of a vampire dog?

Its bite is worse than its bark!

Why did the monster throw up after it ate the priest?

Because it's hard to keep a good man down!

Why wasn't the zombie chosen to teach at the drama school?

They wanted someone more lively!

How do you make a witch scratch herself?

Take away the "w" to make her itch.

What did the vampire say to the invisible man?

Long time, no see!

WHICH MONSTER NEVER USES DEODORANT?

Stankenstein!

Why did the dragon join a gym?

It wanted to burn some calories!

What did the daddy ogre say to his son?

Stop goblin your food!

How does a wizard know what time it is?

He checks his wrist witch!

What advice should you remember if you're running away from a zombie?

Don't go down any dead ends!

Why was the werewolf arrested at the meat counter?

He'd been caught chop-lifting!

WHAT DO YOU CALL A WITCH AT THE SEASIDE?

A sand-witch!

Who saves drowning spirits at the seaside?

The ghostguard!

Why was the swamp monster late for work?

He got bogged down in traffic!

What do you call a haunted hen?

A poultry-geist!

How high do witches fly?

Way up in the atmos-fear!

WHAT DOES A ZOMBIE READ FIRST IN THE NEWSPAPER?

Its horror-scope!

What's the worst game to play with a huge, angry troll?

Squash!

What did the ghost say to the terrified child as it floated across his room?

Don't worry, I'm just passing through!

What type of witch can help you see in the dark?

A lights-witch.

Did you hear about the overworked zombie?

He was dead on his feet!

What do elves use to make their sandwiches?

Shortbread!

Which ice cream do vampires like best?

Vein-illa!

What do you call a friendly pharaoh?

A chummy mummy!

Why do werewolves get good grades at school?

Because they can always come up with a snappy answer!

WHAT GOES "HA HA, THUNK?"

A monster laughing its head off!

How do mummies hide?

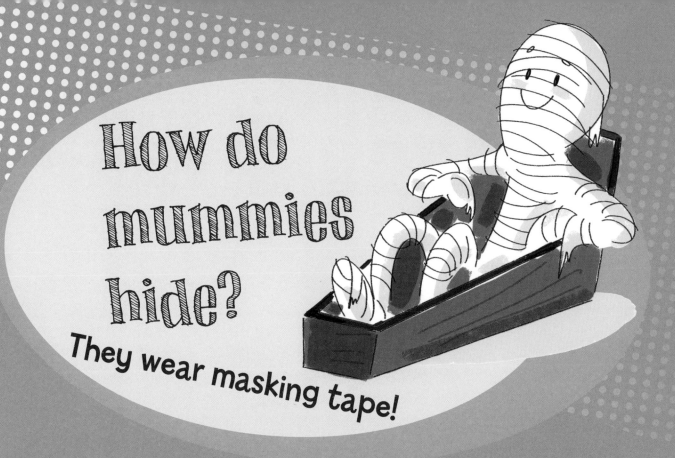

They wear masking tape!

When does a zombie go to sleep?

When it's dead tired!

What do you call a witch at the beach who is too scared to swim?

A chicken sand-witch!

What does a headless horseman ride?

A night-mare!

How do vampires wash themselves?

They get in the bat tub!

WHAT DO YOU CALL A WEREWOLF WITH NO MONEY?

Paw!

Did you hear about the monster that listened to classical music all day?

It had a suite tooth!

Did you hear about the witch in the five-star hotel?

She ordered broom service!

What board game do zombies avoid?

The Game of Life!

What type of potato does Frankenstein like best?

Monster mashed!

What sport does King Kong like to play?

Ping Pong!

What do aliens do to congratulate each other?

They give each other a high six!

What does a monster give her husband on Valentine's day?

Ughs and kisses!

What do you get if you cross a vampire and a criminal?

A fangster!

Where do clever aliens study?

In a parallel university!

Where did Dracula go sightseeing?

The Vampire State Building!

What does an alien use to keep its jeans up?

An asteroid belt!

Have you heard the new joke about the body snatchers?

I'd better not tell it, you might get carried away!

What do you call a dinosaur that's been on a diet?

The Lot Less Monster!

WHY DO YOU NEVER SEE A FAT VAMPIRE?

Because they eat necks to nothing!

What is a zombie most likely to receive a medal for?

Dead-ication!

What time of day do zombies like best?

Ate o'clock!

Which fruit do vampires like to eat?

Neck-tarines!

Which monster lives in the forest?

Franken-pine!

Who goes to ghost school?

Ghoulboys and ghoulgirls!

WHAT DOES A WITCH SAY WHEN SHE'S MADE A CAULDRON FULL OF EYEBALL SOUP?

That should see me through the week!

What does a monster take for a splitting headache?

Superglue!

Does Dracula ever eat steak?

Yes, but very rarely!

What did the werewolf say to the skeleton?

It's been nice gnawing you!

How do you stop a robot from biting its nails?

Replace them with screws!

What do banshees take to the beach?

Sunscream!

What directions did the goblin give to the lost ghost?

Go straight, then make a fright at the next turn!

What do you get if you cross a zombie with a gangster?

Frankenstein's mobster!

How do you reach the second floor of a haunted house?

Climb up the monstairs!

What safety device is found in all ghost cars?

Sheet belts!

What did the vampire say to his dentist?

Fangs very much!

What do skeletons say before each meal?

Bone appetit!

Did you hear about the monster that ate a lamp?

It just wanted a light lunch!

Do monsters eat snacks with their fingers?

No, they eat the fingers separately.

WHY WAS THE MONSTER TOP OF THE CLASS?

Because two heads are better than one!

Why did the vampire teacher suddenly leave class?

She needed to take a coffin break!

How do ghosts make themselves heard in a crowd?

They use a loud-spooker!

Who's in charge of Monster City?

The night-mayor!

What do spooks put their drinks on?

Ghosters.

What happens if a green dragon paddles in the Red Sea?

It gets its feet wet!

WHICH HOLIDAY DO VAMPIRES LIKE BEST?

Fangs-giving!

Why do skeletons find it easy to stay calm?

Because nothing gets under their skin!

Why should you tell jokes to a ghost?

To lift her spirits!

What day of the week do ghosts look forward to?

Fright-day!

How do you greet a four-headed monster?

Hello, hello, hello, hello!

Where should you send a dirty alien?

Into a meteor shower!

Can a monster jump higher than a tree?

Of course it can. Trees can't jump!

Where do the scariest aliens live?

In a far off, distant terror-tory!

Why were the vampires upside down?

They were just hanging out!

WHAT DO YOU CALL AN ALIEN WITH NO EYE? "Alen."

Did you hear about the vampire that preyed on polar bears?

It got frostbite!

Why did the witch have sore knees?

She suffered from broom-atism!

What monster likes cleaning?

The Grim Sweeper!

Did you hear about the poltergeist in the china shop?

It had a smashing time!

Why did the witch put her broom in the washing machine?

She wanted a clean sweep!

Why can't skeletons play hymns in church?

Because they don't have any organs!

What's as sharp and pointed as one of Dracula's fangs?

The other one!

What did the ghost order at the restaurant?

Ghoulash!

What do you get if King Kong sits on your piano?

Flat notes!

What do you get if you cross an undead creature with a shellfish?

Frankenstein's lobster!

What do monsters eat with their sandwiches?

Ghoulslaw!

What do aliens use to shave their faces?

Laser blades!

What party game do monsters like best?

Swallow the leader!

What happened when the girl vampire met the boy vampire?

It was love at first bite!

WHY SHOULD YOU NEVER LIE TO A MONSTER WITH X-RAY VISION?

Because it can see right through you!

What do you call a monster in a toy car? Stuck!

Why do Frankenstein's monster's arms squeak?

Because he ran out of elbow grease!

What's a ghoul's best-loved dessert?

Strawberries and scream!

What's it like to have a monster as a pilot?

Terror-flying!

What happens when a ghost gets lost in fog?

He's mist.

WHAT'S BIG AND UGLY AND BLUE?

A monster holding its breath!

What is William Shakespook's most famous play?

Romeo and Ghouliet!

How do monsters travel on business trips?

By scare-plane!

What game do you play with a baby ghost?

Peeka-boo!

What do vampires do at the circus?

Go for the juggler (the jugular)!

Which sweet treats do aliens like best?

Martian-mallows!

What party game do ghouls play?

Musical scares!

Why don't witches need dictionaries?

Because they're very good at spelling!

How do you stop a werewolf attacking you?

Throw a stick and shout "fetch!"

What do ghosts like to eat for dessert?

I scream!

Why did the one-armed monster go into town?

To visit the second-hand shop!

Why did the girl want to kiss Dracula?

She was batty about him!

Did you hear about the single monster who tried online dating?

She was looking for an edible bachelor!

HOW DO YOU GET A BABY ALIEN TO SLEEP?

Rocket!

Why should a mummy be careful on its day off?

So it doesn't unwind too much!

Where do vampire teachers come from?
Teacher draining school!

Chloe: I wish I had been born a thousand years ago.

Teacher: Why's that?

Chloe: There would be a lot less history to learn!

Teacher: Why were you late this morning?

Alex: Because I saw a sign that said, "School Ahead, Go Slow."

Which city was caught cheating on its exams?

Peking!

WHICH COUNTRY DID THE HUNGRY STUDENT WANT TO STUDY?   Turkey!

What's black and white and hard?

A physics exam!

Teacher: What is the shortest month?

Sarah: May. It only has three letters!

Why is the library a school's tallest building?

Because it has the most stories!

What nation do geography teachers love best?

Expla-nation!

What do you get when you divide the circumference of a jack-o'-lantern by its diameter?

Pumpkin pi!

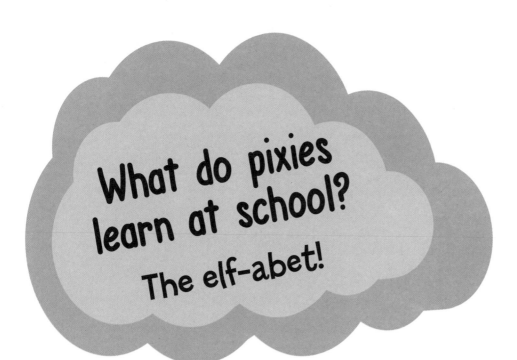

What do pixies learn at school?

The elf-abet!

What did the science teacher say before he got into a fight?

Let me atom!

What did the pencil sharpener say to the pencil?

Stop going around in circles, and get to the point!

Gym teacher: What position do you play?

Bob: I've been told I'm the main drawback, sir.

Teacher: Which of King Arthur's knights invented the round table?

Hailey: Sir Cumference?

Teacher: Have you put clean water in the fish tank?

Bradley: No, it hasn't drunk the first tankful yet!

Dad: Why are your history grades so low?

Lucy: They keep asking about things that happened before I was born!

How long does it take a gymnast to get to class?

A split second!

Why didn't the nose want to go to school?

It got picked on!

What four-letter word becomes longer when you add two

Long!

Which fruit was said to have launched a thousand ships?

Melon of Troy!

What happened at the Boston Tea Party?

I don't know, I wasn't invited!

Teacher: What's the chemical formula for water?

Natalie: HIJKLMNO

Teacher: Wrong!

Natalie: Really? Yesterday you said it was "H to O."

How did the Vikings communicate?

By Norse code!

WHY DID THE SNAKE GET TOLD OFF IN CLASS?

It was always hiss-pering!

What did you learn in school today?

Not enough, I have to go back tomorrow!

Dad: Did you come first in any of your school subjects?

Daisy: No, but I was first out of the classroom when the bell rang!

Why was the clock in the school cafeteria slow?

Because it always went back four seconds.

Teacher: Can you name ten dinosaurs?

Ben: Yes, eight *T. rex* and two *Stegosaurus*.

Miss Addison: Michelle, are those new glasses?

Michelle: Yes, I'm hoping they'll improve di-vision!

DID YOU HEAR ABOUT THE PENCIL WITH AN ERASER ON EACH END?

It's pointless!

Why did the music teacher have to miss school?

He was a trebled man!

Why did the leopard miss so many classes?

He kept breaking out in spots!

Why did the student walk to school facing the wrong way?

It was "back-to-school day"!

Why are grammar teachers superstitious?

They don't want to get bad comma (karma)!

What's worse than finding a worm in your school dinner?

Finding half a worm in your school dinner!

Teacher: When things go wrong, what can you always count on?

Sally: Your fingers?

Why did the girl study in her bedroom instead of the living room?

She wanted a higher education!

Why did the music teacher bring a ladder to class?

So her students could reach the high notes!

Coach: Why didn't you stop the ball?

Goalkeeper: I thought that's what the net was for!

Which subject do pirates like best?

Arrrrt!

What kind of toilet paper do mathematics teachers prefer?

Multi-ply!

Teacher: What stays in the corner but travels around the world?

Anna: A postage stamp!

Which birds are found in Portugal?

Portu-geese!

WHAT DOES AN ENGLISH TEACHER CALL ONE OF SANTA'S ELVES?

A subordinate Claus!

Teacher: Which was the first animal in space?

Louis: The cow that jumped over the Moon?

Why did the science teacher visit a tanning salon?

Because she was a pale-ontologist!

Which snakes are good at equations?

Adders!

Why didn't the Sun attend college?

Because it already had a million degrees!

Sorry I'm late, teacher, I overslept.

What, you mean you sleep at home as well?

WHAT HAPPENED WHEN THE WHEEL WAS INVENTED?

It caused a revolution!

Teacher: Why does your homework look like your dad wrote it?

Emily: Because I used his pen!

Teacher: What's the best thing about school?

Callum: Coming home again!

Teacher: I wish you would pay a little attention.

Jack: I'm paying as little as a I can!

What is a butterfly's best subject?

Moth-ematics!

Which game do tornadoes like best?

Twister!

Why do all classrooms have bright lights?

Because the students are so dim!

Who invented fractions?

King Henry the Fifth!

Art teacher: What shade would you paint a belch?

Rosie: Burple!

Why couldn't the hyphen stay for dinner?

He had to dash!

WHY WAS THE STUDENT LIKE A SEAHORSE?

His grades were all below C-level.

Teacher: Jake, your essay on "My dog" is exactly the same as your sister's.

Jake: I know, Miss Jones. It's the same dog.

What kind of teacher enjoys morning roll call?

The kind that keeps forgetting names!

Teacher: Simon, can you say you name backward?

Simon: No, miss!

What did the bravest Egyptians use for writing?

Hero-glyphics!

What sport do horses like best?

Stable tennis!

English Teacher: Name two pronouns.

Daniel: Who, me?

Which vegetables do librarians like?

Quiet peas!

What did the music teacher say to the two students who wouldn't perform together?

Just duet!

Teacher: What kind of creature is that?

Connor: It's our pet, Tiny.

Teacher: But it's so small. What animal is it?

Connor: It's my-newt!

HOW DO TREES GET ON THE INTERNET?

They log in!

What did the ocean say to the river?

Nothing, it just waved!

Why didn't 4+4 want any dinner?

Because it already 8!

Why was 6 afraid of 7?

Because 7 8 9!

What do a burger and a high school teacher have in common?

They're both pro-teen!

What was carved on a knight's grave if he died in battle?

Rust in peace!

Why was the calendar so popular?

It had a lot of dates!

What did the vegetarian teacher say at lunchtime?

Lettuce eat our salads now!

What do a cookie and a computer have in common?

They both have chips!

Which animal can't be trusted during exams?

The cheetah!

Teacher: How long did the philosopher Aristotle live?

Aaron: All his life!

How do bright students travel when they leave school?

On scholar-ships!

What do Egyptian cheerleaders shout?

Ra Ra Ra!

Girl: Do you know who I am? I'm the principal's daughter.

Boy: Do you know who I am?

Girl: No.

Boy: Good.

WHY DID THE BOY COME FIRST IN THE RACE?

He had athlete's foot!

TeaCHeR: WHeN DiD Caesar reiGN?

Billy: I didn't know he rained. I thought it was "Hail, Caesar."

Why did the art teacher get suspended?

She didn't know where to draw the line!

What is the Great Depression?

It's when you get a bad grade in history!

Teacher: Anyone who hasn't done their homework will be in big trouble.

Joe: How can we get in trouble for something we didn't do?

TeaCHeR: I'd like to go through a whole lesson without telling you off.

Sam: Be my guest.

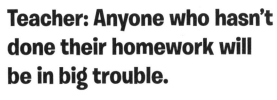

Teacher: Didn't I tell you to stand at the end of the line?

Jamie: I tried, but there was somebody there already!

Why were the early days of history called the Dark Ages?

Because there were so many knights!

Our teacher talks to herself.

So does ours, but she thinks we're listening!

What grades do musicians get?

High Cs!

WHY DID THE MATHEMATICS TEACHER HAVE AN OLD-FASHIONED ALARM CLOCK?

She liked arithma-ticks!

Teacher: Mike, your ideas are like diamonds.

Mike: What, they are beautiful and precious?

Teacher: No, they're extremely rare!

Parent: What did you do at school today?

Son: We played a guessing game.

Parent: I thought you had an arithmetic test?

Son: That's right.

Teacher: Jack, I hope I didn't see you looking at Tyler's exam paper?

Jack: I hope you didn't, too!

What happens to science teachers when they die?

They barium!

Which hand do you write with?

I don't, I write with a pen!

**TEACHER:
IF I HAD 6 APPLES
IN ONE HAND AND 8
APPLES IN THE OTHER,
WHAT WOULD I HAVE?**

Sally: Enormous hands!

What subject do athletes like the best?

Jog-raphy!

How do you cut the ocean in half?

You use a sea-saw!

Teacher: Why haven't you done your science homework?

Luke: Sorry, I'm reading a book on glue, and I just couldn't put it down!

How do bees get to school?

On the school buzz.

Why was everyone locked out of the music room?

Because the keys were on the piano!

Who were the most fierce kings in history?

The Vi-kings!

Why is there lightning in the staff room?

The teachers are brainstorming!

Teacher: You know you can't sleep in my class!

Adam: I think I could if you were a little more quiet!

Why are baby goats so good at long division?

They're smart kids!

Which Roman Emperor suffered from hayfever?

Julius Sneezer!

Why is Britain so wet?

Because the queen has reigned there for so long!

Why did the apostrophe grab all the toys?

It was possessive!

Teacher: What was the Romans' greatest achievement?

Jordan: Learning to speak Latin!

WHY WAS THE SKELETON KEPT BACK A YEAR?

Because it was a numbskull!

Why did the astronaut walk out of class?
It was launch time!

How do you make 1 into 0?

Add a "g" at the beginning, and it's gone!

Dad: How did your exams go?

James: I got almost 10 in every subject!

Dad: Really?

James: Well, I got the zero but not the one.

Dad: And how did the exams go today?

James: I got 100%.

Dad: That's great. Which subjects?

James: 50% in history and 50% in geography.

WHERE DID MEDIEVAL KNIGHTS PARK THEIR CAMELS?

In Camelot!

What tool does an arithmetic teacher use the most?

Multi-pliers!

Teacher: What's the definition of asymmetry?

Student: A place where you bury dead people.

Why didn't Socrates like old French fries?

Because they were made in Ancient Greece!

Why were the first Americans like ants?

Because they lived in colonies!

What kind of hair does Neptune have?

Wavy!

Science teacher: Can anyone please give me a definition of water?

Reece: Yes, I can! It's a clear liquid that turns brown when you put your hands in it.

Teacher: Give me an example of a sentence with the word "detention" in it.

Claire: I had to stop watching a movie last night because I couldn't stand de tension!

Why did the science teacher remove his doorbell?

He wanted to win the no-bell prize!

157

What do history teachers talk about at parties?

The good old days!

What do you call a knight who is afraid to fight?

Sir Render!

Did you hear about the two IT teachers who got married?

It was love at first site!

Why couldn't the student write an essay on fish?

He didn't have any waterproof ink!

WHAT DID THE GEOMETRY TEACHER ORDER FOR DESSERT?

Pi!

Which Egyptian invented the trumpet?
Tooting-khamun!

Did you hear about the archaeological dig for elephant bones?
It was a mammoth task!

Why couldn't the Egyptian god talk?
He was a little Horus.

Why did the school cleaner hate the basketball team?
Because of all the dribbling on court!

What kind of dinosaur knows the most words?
A thesaurus!

WHY WAS THE IT teacher Late For work?

He had a hard drive!

Why did Columbus cross the ocean?

To get to the other tide!

Why aren't there any desks in the mathematics classroom?

Because they use times tables!

Why did the firefly get bad test results?

It wasn't very bright!

Why did the geometry teacher stay home from class?

She'd sprained her angle!

Why is the Pharaoh so big-headed?

Because he Sphinx he's the best!

Teacher: I want you to write an essay on a giraffe.

Ryan: I can't.

Teacher: Why not?

Ryan: I don't have a ladder.

Why are fish so intelligent?

Because they live in schools!

When are you allowed to take bubblegum to school?

On Chews-day!

Why did the teacher write on the window?

Because she wanted her lesson to be clear.

Where did the teacher send the Viking when he felt sick in class?

To the school Norse!

What did the ghost teacher say to the class?

Look at the board, and I will go through it again.

Teacher: Sammy, you missed school yesterday, didn't you?

Sammy: Not really!

Where does the school furniture go to dance?

To the local desk-o!

SCIENCE TEACHER: WHAT HAPPENS IF YOU PUT OXYGEN WITH MAGNESIUM?

Hannah: OMg!

Which subject do snakes like best?
Hiss-tory!

What did the gym teacher do when it began to rain hard?

She turned on the floodlights!

Teacher: Sleep is really good for the brain.

Student: Then why can't we sleep in class?

What school supply does a king like best?

The ruler!

Why did the student go to the arithmetic class?

To make up the numbers!

DID YOU HEAR ABOUT THE UNHAPPY ALGEBRA BOOK? It had too many problems.

Where did the ruler Montezuma study?

At Az Tech.

What did the limestone say to the geologist?

Don't take me for granite!

How do you impress an art teacher?

Easel-y!

How is an English teacher like a judge? They both give out sentences!

Why was it so easy for Sherlock Holmes to learn his alphabet? Because it was L-M-N-try.

Arthur: I took the school bus home yesterday.

Oscar: Really?

Arthur: Yes, but I had to bring it back this morning.

Teacher: Eleven is an odd number, but how do you make it even?

Stacey: Take away the "el"!

WHaT FiSH DOeS a MUSiC TeacHeR LiKe THe BeST?

A piano tuna!

What do you say if your English teacher is crying?

There, their, they're.

How was the Roman Empire divided up?

With a pair of Caesars!

Why do crocodiles get good grades at school?

Because they can always come up with a snappy answer!

If H_2O is the formula for water, what is the formula for ice?

H_2O cubed!

What did one raindrop say to the other?

Two's company, three's a cloud!

What happens if you throw a pile of books into the ocean?

You get a title wave!

There's only one thing worse than taking exams ...

The grades you get afterward.

Teacher: Why were you sent out of tennis class?

Abby: For making a racket!

Why did the school cafeteria hire a dentist?

To make more filling meals!

Teacher: Did you find the exam questions easy?

Nicholas: Oh yes, it was just the answers I found hard.

What kind of cake do you get in the school cafeteria?
A stomach-cake!

Teacher: Do you know why your grades are so bad?

Nathan: I can't think.

Teacher: Exactly!

Matthew: I just banged my head on my desk.

Teacher: Have you seen the school nurse?

Matthew: No, just stars.

What's the relationship between past, present, and future?

Tense!

WHAT'S PURPLE AND 5,000 MILES LONG?
The Grape Wall of China!

How did Benjamin Franklin feel when he discovered electricity?

Shocked!

Why would someone attend night school?

So they can learn to read in the dark!

Why do pirates struggle to learn their alphabet?

Because they get stuck at C!

Teacher: Which animal eats its prey two at a time?

Sophia: Noah's shark!

Why doesn't Frankenstein's monster ever pass his exams?

He hasn't got the brains he was born with!

WHY WAS THE BROOM LATE FOR SCHOOL? It overswept!

Why did the *Archaeopteryx* always catch the worm?

Because it was an early bird!

What is the biggest pencil in the world?

Pennsylvania!

Teacher: What's a computer byte?

Samantha: I didn't even know that it had teeth!

Why don't many people pass the test to become a witch?

Because it's very diff-occult!

Who refereed the tennis match between Caligula and Nero?

The Roman Umpire!

Why was the rodent sent home from school?

He had a bad case of weasels!

Why did the teacher visit the optician?

She couldn't control her pupils!

Teacher: Give me an example of a sentence with the word "counterfeit" in it.

Lily: I wasn't sure if I saw a centipede or a millipede, so I had to counter-feet!

What kind of bus takes you through school, not to school?

A sylla-bus!

What did the paper say to the pencil?

Write on!

What's the fastest country in the world?

Rush-a!

What's the coldest country in the world?

Chile!

Teacher: Have you been stupid all your life?

Andrew: Not yet!

WHY DID THE BOY EAT HIS HOMEWORK?

His teacher said it was a piece of cake!

What do planets like to read?

Comet books.

Why should you never eat breakfast with an alien?

It might contain an Unidentified Frying Object!

Why are aliens green?

Because they're not ripe yet!

What do you call a pattern of stars in the sky that is anxious?

A consternation!

HOW CAN YOU TELL WHEN THE MOON HAS FINISHED ITS DINNER?

Because it's full!

Why couldn't the galaxy find its way home?

Because it didn't know the Milky Way!

If astronauts breathe oxygen during the day, what do they breathe at night?

Night-rogen!

What kind of music do astronauts like?

Rocket 'n' roll!

How can you tell if an alien has used your toothbrush?

It tastes like alien spit!

How do you get a robot to come to a party?

Send it a tin-vitation!

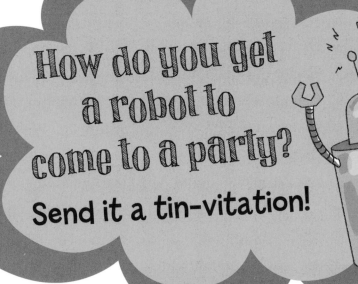

How do robots sit at their desks?

Bolt upright!

What did the girl star say to the boy star?

I really glow for you!

What do you call a bad guy from outer space walking in the sea?

Darth Wader!

Teacher: What is a light-year?

Pupil: The same as a normal year– but with fewer calories?

WHAT DO PLANETS SING AT KARAOKE PARTIES?

Nep-Tunes!

What do you call a piece of gum in space?

A Chew-FO!

What do you call a robot who always goes around obstacles?

R2-Detour!

What's the best way to see flying saucers?

Trip up a waiter!

What do astronauts wear to weddings?

Spacesuits!

Why can't you make a spacecraft out of sandpaper?

Because that would be science friction!

What does Jupiter use to hold up his jeans?

An asteroid belt!

Knock, knock.

Who's there?

Athena.

Athena who?

Athena alien landing in your yard.

Did you hear what happened when my friend Ray attacked an alien?

He became an ex-Ray!

WHAT DO YOU CALL A SET OF TEETH ORBITING A STAR?

A molar system!

How do aliens cook humans?

They like them terri-fried!

Why did Mickey Mouse go to Neptune?

He was looking for Pluto!

What do alien poets write?

Uni-verses!

Where do alien aquatic mammals come from?

Otter space!

Did you hear that Albert Einstein developed a theory about space?

It was about time, too!

179

WHY WOULD AN ALIEN RATHER EAT A SHOOTING STAR THAN AN ASTEROID?

It's a little meteor!

Why didn't the alien eat the clown?

He said it tasted funny!

Planet: Are you joking?

Star: No, I'm Sirius!

Why should you never boil a space telescope?

Because it might Hubble over!

What did the alien cat say when it landed on Earth?

Take me to your litter!

Why are mealtimes on spaceships so popular?

Because the food is out of this world!

What do alien artists paint?

Mars-terpieces!

How do you find an alien with one eye?

It's not easy, you should try using both eyes!

What do you call an alien Santa sled?

A UF-Ho Ho Ho!

How do you get directions in space?

Askeroid!

What drink do aliens like best?

Gravi-tea!

Teacher: Why are you on the floor in front of Buzz Aldrin?

Student: I asked him if he was the first person on the Moon, and he said, "No, Neil before me."

What do you get if you cross a wizard with a spaceship?

A flying sorcerer!

What board game do astronauts like best?

Moon-opoly!

HOW DO YOU KNOW IF AN ALIEN IS JEALOUS?

It turns green!

Why did the astronaut cover his spaceship in mustard?

So the aliens couldn't ketchup with him!

Why did the astronaut build her spaceship out of feathers?

Because she wanted to travel light-years!

What do you call a dishonest spacecraft?

A lying saucer!

How do you ride a space horse?

With a saddle-lite!

How did the astronaut manage to visit the Sun?

He went at night when it wasn't so hot!

WHAT DO ALIENS HAVE FOR LUNCH?
Scream of tomato soup!

What steps should you take if you see an alien?

Large ones!

Teacher: What should you do if you find a spaceman?

Student: Park in it, man!

What kind of horse would you ride on the Moon?

A-pollo pony!

What was the sick alien's temperature?

Absolute zero!

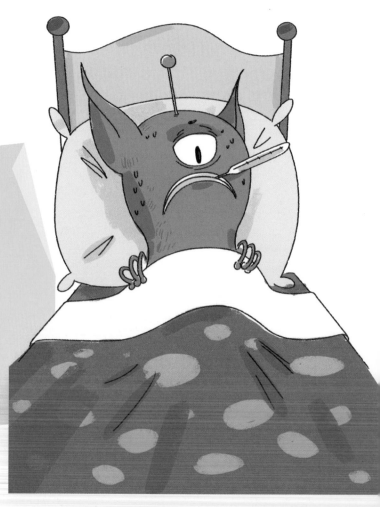

Why can't aliens remember anything?

Because everything goes in one ear and out the others!

Why don't astronauts eat after they take off?

Because they've just had a big launch!

What's sneaky and flies around the Earth?

A subtle-ite!

What do you call alien elocution lessons?

Science diction!

Why is the universe so clean?

Because space is a vacuum!

HOW DO YOU KNOW SATURN IS MARRIED?

You can see its ring!

What do you call an insect on the Moon?

A lunar-tick!

Why is Mercury bald?

Because it has no 'air!

What keyboard key do astronauts use the most?

The space bar!

Why doesn't Luke Skywalker use a spoon?

Because he likes to use the forks!

What's the weakest part of space?

The puny-verse!

Why do astronauts wear bulletproof vests?

To protect themselves against shooting stars!

Where do aliens go to study?

VERY high school!

Where do they go after that?

Universe-ity!

What do you call an insect in a spaceship?

An astron-ant!

DO ROBOTS HAVE BROTHERS?

No, just transistors!

I'd tell you a joke about space, but it's too out of this world!

Did you hear about the alien who wondered where the Sun went at night?

Eventually, it dawned on him!

What do you call a bad guy from outer space who is never on time?

Darth Later!

Why are meteors very good at soccer?

Because they're shooting stars!

What did the alien race car driver say when it landed on Earth?

Take me to your speeder!

Which Egyptian pharaoh was also an astronaut?

Tutanka-moon!

What sweet treats do aliens like best?

Martian-mallows!

What did the astronaut name his dog?

Moon Rover!

Where can you leave your spaceship when visiting a planet?

At a parking meteor!

Why do some aliens have twisted spaceships?

So they can travel at warp speed!

What do aliens drink their space soda from?

Sunglasses!

What advice should you always give to robots?

Look before you bleep!

HOW DO YOU WIN A ROUND OF SPACE GOLF?

With a black hole in one!

How do astronauts like their ice cream?

In floats!

Why shouldn't you be scared of a six-legged alien?

It's 'armless!

What do you call a shooting star that misses the Earth?

A meteor-wrong!

What do you call a rodent that's gone to outer space?

A mouse-tronaut!

What do you get if you cross a robot with a comet?

An aster-droid!

How can you tell the Earth and the Moon are friends?

Because they've been going around together for years!

Where do astronauts keep their sandwiches?

In their launch-boxes!

What do you call a group of freezing planets?

A polar system!

HOW DO YOU KNOW IF THERE'S AN ALIEN IN YOUR HOUSE?

There'll be a spaceship parked in front!

Where do you keep alien fish?

In a planetarium!

What's the difference between a rocket and a fly?

A rocket can fly, but a fly can't rocket!

Where did the Apollo astronauts go to study?

A Moon-iversity!

Why did the asteroid stop trying?

He didn't have enough comet-ment!

How do astronauts see in the dark?

They turn on the satellite!

WHAT DOES THE MOON DO WHEN HIS HAIR GETS TOO LONG?

Eclipse it!

What do you call a bowl of melted chocolate flying through space?

A flying saucer!

What streaks across the night sky going "kapow, kapow"?

A shooting star!

What is the stupidest object in the night sky?

The Fool Moon!

What do astronomers use to keep their valuables safe?

Hubble wrap!

Why did the aliens land at the sports club?

So they could use their tennis rocket!

What did the planet say to the selfish star?

Not everything revolves around you!

Why was the alien bad at dancing?

It had three left feet!

Why did the spacecraft land a rover on Mars?

Just out of Curiosity!

How do you tip over a spaceship?

Rocket!

Why did the asteroid laugh at the shooting star?

It thought it was comet-y!

How can you tell if the Sun is happy?

It's beaming!

Why did the astronaut fly into the black hole?

He didn't understand the gravity of the situation!

How do aliens count to 50?

On their fingers!

HOW DO YOU ORGANIZE A SPACE PARTY?

You planet!

What do you call a really scary alien?

An extra-terror-estrial!

Why should you never trust atoms?

They make up everything!

How does an alien phone the Sun?

It uses a Sun-dial!

Why did the aliens call their baby Jupiter?

Because it was dense and gassy!

What do you call a pattern of stars in the sky that feels sorry for you?

A consolation!

First alien: Do you like people?
Second alien: Yes, but I can only eat a few at a time.

Why couldn't the black hole pass its exams?
Because it's super dense!

What do you call a spaceship covered in sugar and vinegar?
A sweet-and-sour saucer!

What did the alien plant say when it landed on Earth?
Take me to your weeder!

What did the lunar astronauts say when they bumped into each other?
I Apollo-gize!

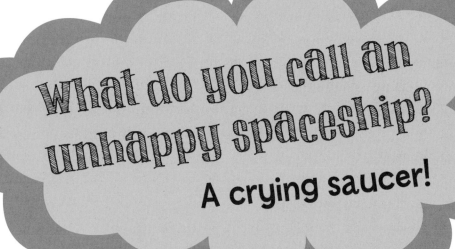

What do you call an unhappy spaceship?

A crying saucer!

Teacher: How many balls of string would it take to reach the Moon?

Student: One, but it'd have to be a really big one!

What do astronomers take to relax?

A Hubble bath!

What do aliens call junk food?

Unidentified Frying Objects!

Where do aliens do their gardening?

In greenhouses!

What does an oversized alien wear?

A not-very-much-space suit!

What do nuclear scientists have for dinner?

Fission chips!

Which star do you get if you crush an insect?

Betelgeuse!

WHAT DO YOU CALL A GLASS ROBOT?

See-Through PO!

What did the alien robot say to the fuel pump?

Take your finger out of your ear when I'm talking to you!

Why are astronauts ambitious?

Because they want to go up in the world!

Why aren't astronauts practical?

Because they are not very down-to-earth people!

Which chocolate bar do astronauts like best?

Mars bars!

Why can't the Sun sing?

Because it's not a rock star!

WHY DID THE SUN GO TO SCHOOL?

To get brighter!

What did the star who came last in the shining brightly competition get?

The constellation prize!

What do alien children do at Halloween?

They go from door to door dressed as humans!

What do you call a a bad guy from outer space who disappears?

Darth Fader!

What do you call a food-loving spaceman?

A gastronaut!

Where do astronauts go to learn how to fly in the darkness of space?

Night school!

Where can you find black holes?

In black socks!

Did you hear about the astronaut who was reading a book on antigravity?

It was impossible to put down!

What do space monsters call humans?

Breakfast, lunch, and dinner!

Why did the astronomer change his mind about the Sun after looking at it through an ultraviolet telescope?

He saw it in a whole different light!

WHAT'S IN THE MIDDLE OF JUPITER?

The letter "i"!

What do you call a noisy spaceship?

A space racket!

What do you call a genuine spacecraft?

A True-FO!

204

What do aliens use to decorate their cakes?

Mars-ipan!

How can you tell Mars has a lot of books?

Because it looks well red!

Did you hear about the cow astronaut?

She landed on the Mooooon!

Did you hear about the satellite dishes that got married?

They had an amazing reception!

What do you call a recently built spaceship?

A New-F-O!

WHY ARE ALIENS SO GOOD AT GARDENING?

Because they have green fingers and thumbs!

Knock, knock.

Who's there?

Jupiter.

Jupiter who?

Jupiter spaceship on my lawn?

What's the best way to talk to aliens?

From a long way away!

What films do alien insects like?

Sci-fly movies!

Which side of a spaceship passes closest to the Moon?

The outside!

What did the hungry alien say when it landed on Earth?

Take me to your feeder!

What do you get if you cross a towel with a spaceship?

A drying saucer!

Teacher: What's closer, the Moon or China?

Student: The Moon, because I can see the Moon at night from here, but I can't see China.

WHICH DANCE DOES NEIL ARMSTRONG LIKE BEST?

The Moon Walk!

What do you say to an alien with two heads?

Hello to you, and hello to you, too!

Why are alien kitchens always very messy?

Because of all the flying sauces!

How many ears does Captain Kirk have?

Three: a right ear, a left ear, and a final frontier!

What do you call a space telescope that doesn't work?

Hubble trouble!

What do you call an alien with three eyes?

An Aliiien!

Why aren't parties on the Moon any fun?

There isn't much atmosphere!

What did the planet say to the star?

You're looking stellar!

How did the alien tie its shoelaces?

With an astro-knot!

Why couldn't the alien book a room on the Moon?

Because it was full!

What do you call two spaceships flying together at exactly the same speed?

Tying saucers!

Why did Darth Vader cross the road?

To get to the Dark Side!

What did Jupiter say to Saturn?

Give me a ring sometime!

Why are aliens good for the environment?

Because they're so green!

What's the most important quality needed to become an astronaut?

A good altitude!

WHY DOESN'T THE SUN NEED TO GO TO COLLEGE?

Because it has a million degrees!

WHAT DO YOU CALL AN ALIEN WEARING PLATFORM HEELS?

A Shoe-FO!

What do you call a Jedi knight in a bubble bath?

Soapy-Wan Kenobi!

What do shooting stars say when they greet each other?

Please to meteor!

Which weighs the most, a full moon or a half moon?

A half moon because the full moon is much lighter!

What did the alien tree say when it landed on Earth?

Take me to your cedar!

WHY DiDN'T THE DOG STAR LAUGH AT THE JOKE?

It was too Sirius!

Why did the astronaut throw eggs at the alien?

He wanted to eggs-terminate it!

What do you call the lights on a lunar spacecraft?

Moonbeams!

What do astronauts put in their sandwiches?

Launch-meat!

What do astronomers like to chew?

Hubble gum!

How should you serve tea to an alien?

On a flying saucer!

What should you do if you see an angry alien?

Give it some space!

What kind of fish live in space?

Nep-tuna!

What do you get if you cross a rocket and a lamb?

A space sheep!

What other kind of fish live in space?

Starfish!

How do aliens play badminton?

With a space shuttlecock!

Knock knock.

Who's there?

Saturn.

Saturn who?

Saturn front of this spaceship, waiting for it to take off!

What do you call a spaceship that doesn't mind its own business?

A prying saucer!

Where do alien fish come from?

Trouter space!

WHAT DO ALIENS CALL ASTRONAUTS IN SPACESHIPS?

Canned food!

What did the dentist say to the golfer?

"I'm afraid you have a hole in one!"

Doctor, I keep thinking I'm Mozart!

I'll be with you in a minuet.

What did the ninja say to the doctor?

Hi-ya!

Doctor, I swallowed a bone.

Are you choking?

No, I really did!

HOW DID THE COMPUTER CATCH A COLD?

It left its Windows open!

Which is faster, hot or cold?

Hot, because anyone can catch a cold!

Why did the stand-up comedian go to see the doctor?

He was feeling a little bit funny!

Why did the snake visit the pharmacist?

It needed some asp-irin!

Doctor, first my sister was obsessed with Tangled, now she's totally into Frozen.

How long has she suffered from these Disney spells?

Why did the germ cross the microscope?

To get to the other slide!

Doctor, I feel like a well. We must get to the bottom of this!

What did the midwife say when she delivered quads?

Four crying out loud!

Doctor, I'm suffering from really bad deja vu!

Didn't I see you yesterday?

Doctor, I keep running around pretending to be a seabird.

No wonder you're puffin!

DOCTOR, I'M SO SORRY I'M LATE, I SPRAINED MY ANKLE ON THE WAY HERE!

That's a lame excuse.

What did one toilet say to the other toilet?

You look flushed!

Did you hear about the pig that lost its voice?

It was disgruntled!

Why did the robot never feel sick?

It had a cast iron stomach!

How do you treat an alien with claustrophobia?

Give it some space!

Doctor, I've swallowed a pen. What should I do?

Use a pencil.

WHY DIDN'T THE BOY TELL THE DOCTOR HE'D SWALLOWED SOME GLUE?

His lips were sealed!

What did the doctor say was wrong with the car mechanic?

He'd had a breakdown!

The mechanic asked for a second opinion.

"Okay," said the other doctor. "You're over-tired."

The mechanic told his wife what the doctors had said.

"Hmm," she agreed. "You do seem exhausted."

What did the doctor say to the volcano?

You need to quit smoking!

Why did the nurse tiptoe past the medicine cabinet? He didn't want to wake the sleeping pills!

Excuse me, what's the quickest way to the hospital?
Lie down on that busy road over there!

How do you know if an aquatic mammal is ill?
They have a high beaver!

Doctor, what did the X-ray of my head show?
Absolutely nothing!

What's worse than a hippo with a cold?
A giraffe with a sore throat!

WHAT DO YOU GIVE TO AN AILING CITRUS FRUIT?

Lemon-aid!

Doctor, I feel like a piece of cake!

Yes, you do look a bit crummy.

What can you catch but never throw?

A cold!

What award does the dentist of the year receive?

A little plaque!

Doctor, I think I need glasses.

I agree, this is a fast-food restaurant.

Why did the bee go to the doctor? Because she had hives!

Doctor, my snoring is so bad, I'm keeping myself awake!

I think you had better sleep in another room!

Doctor, I keep comparing things with something else! Don't panic, it's just analogy.

Who do warlocks see when they are feeling sick? The witch doctor!

Doctor, I keep thinking I'm a bridge! What's come over you? One large truck and six cars!

What happened when William Shakespeare visited the doctor for his cold?

The doc said it was much achoo about nothing!

Did you hear about the moody dentist?

He was always looking down in the mouth!

Doctor, I have no energy. I can't even walk down the road without getting tired.

It's because you're wearing loafers!

WHY DIDN'T THE CHIMNEY FEEL VERY WELL?

It had the flue!

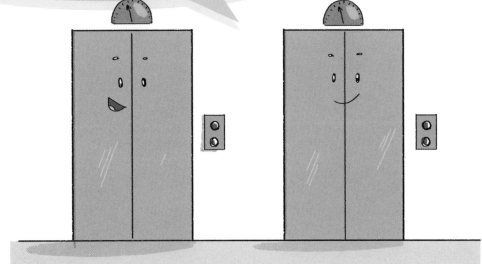

What did one elevator say to the other?

I think I'm coming down with something!

What did the doctor pack for her trip to the desert?

A thirst-aid kit!

What's the medical name for a fear of Santa Claus?

Claus-trophobia.

Doctor, how can I stop my nose from running?

Put your foot out, and trip it up!

Doctor, my stomach hurts after eating crabs.

Did they smell bad when you took them out of their shells?

What do you mean "when I took them out of their shells"?

DOCTOR, I THINK I'M AN ADDER!

Great, can you help with my accounts?

Why was the computer virus so serious?

It was terminal!

Doctor, I keep getting pains in my eye when I drink hot chocolate.

Have you tried taking the spoon out of your mug?

Did you hear about the girl who was smacked in the face by a frisbee?

She wondered why it was getting bigger ... and then it hit her!

Did you hear about the man who swallowed his money?

The doctor was looking for signs of change.

A sheep went to see the vet. "I feel like I always have a cloud hanging over me!"

"Ah," said the vet. "It's because you're always under the weather."

Doctor, no matter what I do, I just can't get to sleep!

Lie on the edge of the bed, and you'll soon drop off.

Doctor, I think I'm a dog!

How long have you felt like this?

Ever since I was a puppy!

Doctor, I don't think these pills you gave me for heavy sweating are working.

Why not?

They keep falling out from under my arms!

How do you make a tissue dance?

Put a little boogie in it!

Why did the monster feel sick?

It had eaten some vegetables!

Doctor, I feel like a wigwam or a tepee all the time!

That just means you're too tents.

Doctor, I keep stealing things!

Hmm, have you taken anything for it?

Did you hear the joke about the germs?

I don't want you to spread it around!

TEACHER: HOW MANY KNEES DO YOU HAVE?

Student: Four! A left knee, a right knee, and two kidneys!

Did you hear about the man who swallowed uranium?

He got atomic ache!

What's green and jumpy?

A frog with hiccups!

Doctor, there's a man who urgently needs you to tend to scratches all over his body.

What's his name?
Claude!

Doctor, I keep thinking I'm a mosquito.

Don't be such a sucker!

Why did the rocket visit the doctor?

To get its booster shot!

WHAT'S THE BEST TIME TO GO TO THE DENTIST?

Tooth-hurty (2:30)!

What did the dentist say when her plane hit turbulence?

Brace yourself!

What did the boat's captain do when he was sick?

He went in to see the dock!

Doctor, I feel like a spoon.

Lie down and don't stir.

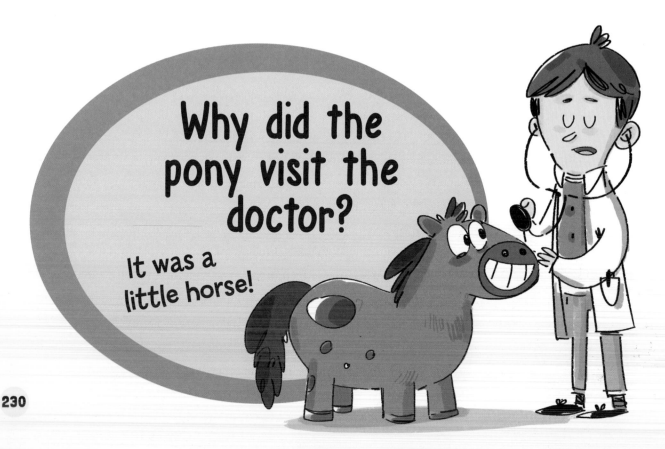

Why did the pony visit the doctor?

It was a little horse!

Why did the ninja spend a week in bed?

He had kung flu!

Doctor, I keep thinking I'm a woodworm.

How boring for you!

Did you hear about the frog that got taken to the mental hospital?

It was hopping mad!

Did you hear about the gardener who had a cold?

He caught it from the germ-aniums!

Did you hear about the artist who was pinned to the ground by wooden frames?

He'd come down with easels!

Why did the chicken visit the doctor?

It was feeling fowl!

Doctor, I keep thinking I'm a python.

You can't get around me just like that, you know.

What did the left eye say to the right eye?

Between you and me, something smells!

What did the bucket say to the baby bucket?

You look a little pail!

DOCTOR, I KEEP THINKING I'M INVISIBLE. Who said that?

Why did the computer cough and sneeze?

It had a virus!

Doctor, I've got an ingrowing toenail, toothache, and halitosis.

Hmm, it sounds like foot and mouth disease.

How do you know if you're cross-eyed?

When you can see eye to eye with yourself!

Doctor, can I get a second opinion?

Of course you can. Come back at the same time tomorrow.

What do dentists call their X-rays?

Tooth pics!

Did you hear about the man who lost his left side in an accident?
Don't worry, he's alright now!

Why are the tonsils excited?

They've heard the doctor is taking them out on Friday!

Why did the tired athlete run around and around her bed?

To catch up on some sleep!

Why did the miniature tool go to see the doctor?

It was a little saw.

WHAT DO YOU CALL A SICK CROCODILE?

An illigator!

Why did the van bounce down the road?

It was a hiccup truck!

What TV shows do germs hate?

Soap operas!

How do you take a pig to the local hospital?

In a hambulance!

What did the judge say to the dentist?

Do you swear to pull the tooth, the whole tooth, and nothing but the tooth?

Doctor, I keep dreaming I'm an apple. We need to get to the core of this.

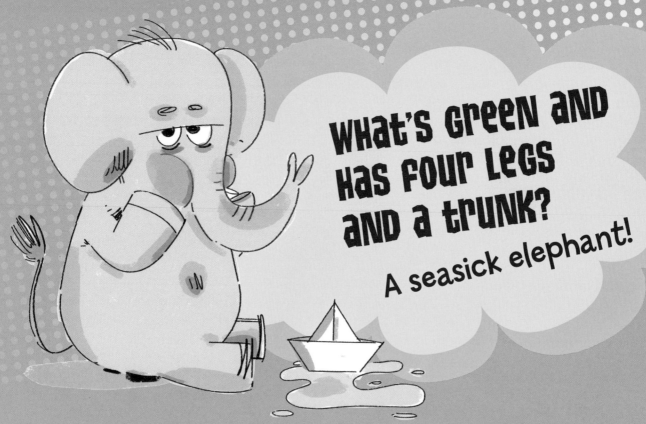

WHAT'S GREEN AND HAS FOUR LEGS AND A TRUNK?

A seasick elephant!

What does the queen do if she burps?

She issues a royal pardon!

Why did the carpenter see a psychiatrist?

He had a screw loose!

Doctor, I keep thinking I'm a fish!

You poor sole.

Doctor, I think I've broken my arm in two places.

Well, don't go back there again.

Doctor, I keep thinking I'm a large ape.

OK, I'm going to need to gorilla you for some answers!

Why did the train worker get an electric shock?

He was the conductor!

My dad keeps shouting out: "A! E! I! O! U!"

It sounds like he has irritable vowel syndrome.

What did the doctor prescribe for the pig?

Oinkment.

Doctor, I keep eating nuts, bolts, and screws.

That's riveting!

How was the blind carpenter suddenly cured?

He picked up his hammer and saw!

What do you call a sick extraterrestrial?

An ailin' alien!

Doctor, I feel like a sheep.

That's baaaaad!

Doctor, I feel funny.

That's hardly surprising–you look hilarious!

DID YOU HEAR ABOUT THE FROG THAT HAD A BREAKDOWN?

It got toad away!

What's the best way to stop your nose from running?

Stand on your head!

Doctor, I really feel like a carrot, what should I do?

Well, don't get in a stew.

Doctor, I keep thinking I'm a yo-yo.

Are you trying to string me along?

A horse went to the doctor: "I sleep all day, and then I'm awake all night."

"You sound like a night-mare!"

Doctor, I keep thinking I'm a horse!

Take one of these pills every four hours, with hay.

DOCTOR, I'M really afraid THAT I'VE TURNED INTO A VAMPIRE.

Necks, please!

Doctor, I feel like a cup of tea.

Excellent idea, make me one, too!

Doctor, I keep thinking I'm the king of the jungle.

I think you're lion.

What did the alien say when it needed blood tests?

Take me to your bleeder!

Why can't a nose be twelve inches long?

Because then it would be a foot!

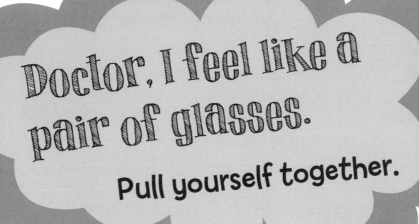

Doctor, I feel like a pair of glasses.

Pull yourself together.

Did you hear about the dentist who went to the Arctic?

It was a molar expedition!

Did you hear about the truck driver with depression?

He had to pull over for a shoulder to cry on!

Doctor, I can't walk properly. I keep jumping everywhere!

Have you been feeling a bit up and down?

Why did the mummy think it had a cold?

Because of its coffin!

241

What did the doctor prescribe for the pony?

Cough stirrup!

The pony's cough is worse.

What do we do?

We take it to a horse-pital!

Why was the mink sent home from school?

It had a bad case of weasels!

Doctor, I think I've been put together all wrong!

Why do you think that?

Because my feet smell and my nose runs!

DOCTOR, MY NOSE IS ALL RED AND LOOKS LIKE A STRAWBERRY.

Here you go, put this cream on it.

Why did the deer visit the dentist?

He needed his buck teeth fixed!

If an athlete suffers from athlete's foot, what does a soldier suffer from?

Missile-toe!

Doctor: You need new glasses.

Patient: How do you know?

Doctor: I could tell as soon as you walked through the window.

Which subject did the dentist get an A in at school?

Flossophy!

Doctor, I think I'm becoming invisible.

Yes, I can see that you're not all there.

Doctor, I've lost my memory!

When did that happen?

When did what happen?

What did the sailor say as he threw up on a windy day?

It's all coming back to me now!

What can run but can't walk?

Your nose!

Doctor, my monkey doesn't like his medicine.

Tell him he'll get what he's gibbon.

What type of fish causes indigestion?

A stomach hake!

What do you get if you cross a comedian and germs?

A sick joke!

Doctor, everyone keeps ignoring me.

Next, please!

What do you call a pig lying in the Sun?

Bacon!

DOCTOR, I THINK I'M A BELL. WHAT SHOULD I DO?

Take this medicine, and if nothing changes, give me a ring!

Did you hear about the man who was hit on the head by an icicle?

It knocked him cold!

Did you hear the joke about bad breath?

It stinks!

Doctor, I keep thinking I'm a nit.

Will you please get out of my hair!

What do you give sick insects?

Anty-biotics!

DOCTOR, HELP! I THINK I'M SHRINKING!

Wait there, and be a little patient.

246

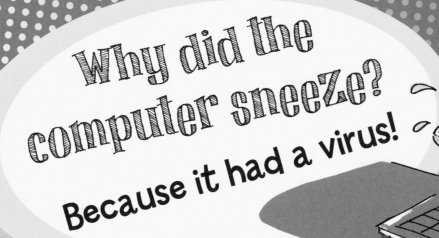

Why did the computer sneeze?

Because it had a virus!

What does a doctor give to an elephant with a vomiting bug?

Plenty of room!

Did you hear about the frog with the broken leg?

It was feeling unhoppy!

Doctor, I keep thinking I'm a caterpillar.

Don't worry, you'll soon change.

What did the doctor say to the sick bodybuilder?

Take a seat in the weighting room.

DOCTOR, I KEEP THINKING I'M A WASP!

Buzz off, and stop bothering me!

What does a nut say when it sneezes?

Cashew!

Did you hear about the thief who went to the doctor because she couldn't sleep?

The doctor gave her a mat and told her to lie low for a while.

Where do people get their medicine in the countryside?

From a farmer-cist!

Doctor, I keep thinking I'm a spider.

Sounds like a web of lies to me.

Why did the house visit the doctor?

It had a window pain!

Doctor, I keep hearing a ringing sound!

Then answer your phone, silly!

When does a doctor get angry?

When she runs out of patients!

Doctor, I feel like I'm a sharp pencil.

I see your point!

DID YOU HEAR ABOUT THE BEAR THAT ENDED UP IN A HOSPITAL?

It had a grizzly accident!

Why did the pie go to the dentist?

It needed a filling!

Doctor, everything I touch turns to gold!

Don't worry, it's just a gilt complex.

What's the best cure for graphite poisoning?

Pencil-lin!

Why did the headless ghost go to see the doctor?

Because he wasn't all there!

A man goes to see the doctor. He has a cucumber in one ear, a breadstick in the other ear, and a banana up his nose. The doctor knows instantly what is wrong.

"You're not eating properly!"

What's a dentist's top attraction at the amusement park?

The "fluor-ride!"

Why did the dentist keep falling asleep?

Because drilling teeth is boring!

Why was the doctor worried about the obese alien?

It was an extra-cholesterol!

Why do you feel down in the mouth when you have a cold?

Because your nose is off-scenter!

What should you do when an elephant catches a cold?

Stand back!

Did you hear about the witch who turned green?

She got broom sick on long journeys!

Doctor, I keep thinking that I'm a dog!

Climb up on the couch, and I'll take a look at you.

But I'm not allowed on the couch!

Doctor, would you say I have a split personality?

One at a time, please!

Doctor, everyone thinks I'm a liar.

I can't believe that!

DID YOU HEAR ABOUT THE PIG THAT WENT ON A PLANE?

Swine flu!

My mother's a dreadful dancer. She has two left feet.

My mother's like that, too. The doctor told her to wear flip-flips.

How do psychiatrists greet each other?

You are fine. How am I?

Doctor, I'm so confused. Please help me out!

Certainly, the door is there on your left.

Doctor, the Invisible Man is here for his appointment.

Tell him I can't see him now.

Doctor, I keep seeing an insect circling my head.

Don't worry. That's just a bug that's been going around.

WHY DID THE CLOWN CALL THE DOCTOR?

Because he broke his funny bone!

Why did the king visit the dentist?

To get his teeth crowned!

Doctor, I always dream there are monsters under the bed.

Saw the legs off the bed, and you'll be fine!

Doctor, I keep thinking I'm an electric eel.

That's shocking!

Doctor, I dreamed last night that I'd turned into a deck of cards.

I'll deal with you later!

What's red and thick?

A blood clot!

What did the dermatologist say to the frog?

People will learn to love you, warts and all!

Doctor, I keep thinking I've turned into a frog.

What's so bad about that?

I'm afraid I might croak!

Doctor, I think I'm a very shy snail.

Don't worry, we'll soon bring you out of your shell.

What noise did the train make when it had a cold?

Aaaa-choo-choo!

Why did the doctor send the vampire to the nurse?

For blood tests!

When should you go to see a bird doctor?

When you're puffin!

What did the doctor give to the bird with a sore throat?

Tweetment!

Doctor, my brother thinks he's an escalator.

Tell him to come and see me.

I can't, he doesn't go up to this floor.

WHAT DID THE LITTLE BROOM SAY TO THE BIG BROOM?

I just can't get to sweep!